LOSING SAMMY

Letters through a miscarriage

Valerie Theng

Losing Sammy - Letters through a miscarriage

Published in 2012 by 10Publishing, a division of 10ofthose.com

9D Centurion Court, Farington, Leyland, PR25 3UQ

Email: info@10ofthose.com
Website: www.10ofthose.com

ISBN: 978-1-906173-91-3

Design by Diane Bainbridge
Printed and bound by CPI Group (UK) Ltd, Croydon, England, CR0 4YY

DEDICATION

To Josh

You would not let it go until my voice found its way, and my heart came to rest.

10 Publishing
a division of 10 of those.com

Losing Sammy is most helpfully written. Each of Valerie's eleven letters finishes with an upward glance, reassuring the reader of a loving, ever present God, who can only be, and is always faithful. Having read these letters, I now realise, that what I felt twenty two years ago was 'normal'. Grief is a journey. I like Valerie, look forward to heaven, when I will be able to love my unborn child and will understand in full, God's perfect sovereignty. This is where Valerie's book so wisely and comfortingly ends - with another upward glance!

Jane Rowlands

No-one really talks about miscarriages; it's something you're expected to deal with quietly. I read this book shortly after my third miscarriage and to read what Valerie had written in her raw stage of grief was just what I needed. To know that someone else has felt what you're feeling is so reassuring. And even if you haven't had a miscarriage, reading this will help you understand how those who have are feeling. A much needed resource.

Jenny Brake

PART TIME ILLUSTRATOR AND FULL TIME MUM

If you are bearing the loss and heartbreak of miscarriage, let Valerie Theng walk that road with you. Written with searing honesty and deep empathy, Valerie's heartfelt letters will remind you of God's love and faithfulness, and help you see glimmers of hope and healing in the darkness. If you haven't experienced miscarriage personally, then this book is also for you! Reading Valerie's record of her journey through grief will help you understand, support and care for others who know the pain of miscarriage themselves.

Kate Lewis

MINISTER'S WIFE BASED IN LEYLAND, ENGLAND

Many of us will be called to pastor and care for those who are journeying through the grief of a miscarriage. Often we are unsure of what to do or say. Through these letters, we are helped to understand how we can lament with those who are wounded. The voices are refreshingly raw and honest, giving us insight into hearts that mourn. And yet, through the deep sorrows, we hear words of compassion and comfort. This book helps us, and those we minister to, find shelter in the warm embrace of our heavenly Father.

John Russell

MINISTER, CORNERSTONE CHURCH, NOTTINGHAM, ENGLAND

Miscarriage is rarely talked about and as a midwife I have spent many painful hours with grieving women. It is an invisible pain and one that many find very difficult to discuss. Valerie Theng's honest and brave account of her own personal heartbreak of losing her child conveys the journey that many women travel along. However, the hope that Valerie gives through this book is the only hope that we all have to help us through the struggles of this earthly life in that God, who also knows the pain of loss in the death of His Son Jesus Christ, is the ultimate Healer.

Lorraine Gosling

NHS MIDWIFE BASED IN THE NORTH EAST OF ENGLAND

CONTENTS

Preface 11

Introduction 13

My Private Laments to the Lord 16

Letter One: Death 19

Letter Two: The Emptying 26

Letter Three: Recuperating 29

Letter Four: Truth Telling 34

Letter Five: Here Comes the Rain 40

Letter Six: Hiding 46

Letter Seven: Taking Control 52

Letter Eight: Sharing an Umbrella 57

Looking Back on *Letter Nine* 61

Letter Nine: Over the Rainbow 65

Letter Ten: One Year On 67

Letter Eleven: Dreaming 71

Letter Twelve: To My Beloved Sammy 76

PREFACE

In January 2009, I suffered a miscarriage that would change my world-view and my life. It was unexpected, and left me bewildered. Although I had trained and worked as a therapist, I could not find the means to console myself. I wrote this collection of letters, imagining an unnamed mother whom I might share a moment of sorrow with. This turned in to an eighteen-month long project where I wrote my deepest feelings and most private thoughts.

At the time I miscarried, I was already a mother of two. I dare say that the taste of grief would be different for different women. There are those whom I have spoken to who lost their first child. There are those I spoke with who had lost several babies. Although the circumstances differed, what struck me was the silent anguish each mother felt but rarely expressed. The profound feelings of loss, felt almost immediately after the news was given to them, were often not validated. These torrents of emotions were left to dissipate on their own, each mother relying on private prayer, and hoping the course of time would ease the pain.

I cannot imagine for others what that initial period of loss looked like, or felt like. However, I can offer my story as a means of comfort, to simply say, 'You are not alone.' If you are a spouse, a friend, a relative or a counsellor who has picked up this booklet, then I offer you a window into the heart of grief after a miscarriage; an opportunity to journey with a grieving mother, and perhaps become slightly enlightened yourself.

Our heavenly Father is indeed a gracious and loving God. Although these letters were initially written with surging pain, I rejoice to tell you that I am finally at peace. My Lord has indeed caused me to sing and dance again. The season of grief has passed, and I am sure it will too for those who begin their journey with me in my time of grief. For He is more than able.

Blessings upon blessings!

Valerie Theng

INTRODUCTION

Dear friend,

If you are reading this because you have personally suffered the pain of miscarriage, then my letter has reached you in your time of sadness. As I write, I reach out to you with a blanket of words in your time of grief. It would not be enough to say that I am sorry for your loss and your pain. It would be wrong to say that I understand completely how you feel. This time is yours to grieve. It is your personal pain. It is a journey into suffering. I pray that you will walk with our Father God. It is He who will understand with the completeness of one whom has suffered death and loss.

If you feel a sense of loss, then it is likely you grieve as a mother. Your body held another life within you. For a short, precious time, you witnessed the miracle of creation implanted in you. You know what it is to love a child you have not held. You know what it is to have hoped, anticipated, and longed for your beloved.

You knew what it was to feel fierce protection for your baby. I expect you would have tried something to hold that child back into you. In your instincts and prayerful cries, you were a mother. I use the term 'grief' freely and without shame. We have faced the death of a life. We traversed the turning of the tide, when our joy turned to despair, and then to sadness. We are mothers who loved and lost.

I wrote these letters during the time of my grieving. This collection came about because I yearned to have someone travel with me in my confusion and mourning. I longed to have another woman beside me; someone who was experiencing what I was going through. Most women who had suffered a miscarriage could only tell me what they thought and felt in retrospect. Their stories were embellished by a hope I was not yet ready to embrace. Their wounds had largely healed. Some did not seem to have grieved at all. Most had moved on, and forgotten how it felt. They had forgotten what it was like, moment by moment, to be in the fog. As the miscarriage revealed more about my vulnerabilities and insecurities than I cared to embrace, I searched for a book I could read – not a manual on how to feel or what to do. I did not find it. So I decided to write my letters to you. These are letters written in my time of grief for *you*, in *your* time of grief. As they come from a wound, they are fresh, raw and honest. Sometimes I worried that you might find my words indulgent. I considered if I should wait until my own pain ceased before I wrote. I do not have the answers to these worries. I am not yet appeased. I rest on the certainty that if we were to have met on a rainy day in a café somewhere, at the same time of our grief, then these are the laments and cries we would have shared.

Grief, I think, manifests differently for different people. I expect there will be some letters that disquiet you, and some which console you. In those moments, I hope that you turn to Jesus to make sense of the myriad of thoughts and feelings evoked.

May the Lord watch over you, as your season of grief unfolds.

Love, *Valerie*

MY PRIVATE LAMENTS TO THE LORD

Father, I lost a child today. Did You see him? What was he like? For if You saw him, and You knew him, that makes him real. He existed. If he existed, then my grief is real. The pain I feel exists. Then in that pain I allow myself to sorrow. I whisper my sorrow to You. How quickly the whisper turns to groans. My anguish wells up to one continuous moan. Father! I lost a child today! Did You see him? What was he like?

For You created my inmost being;
You knit me together in my
mother's womb.

(Ps. 139:13)

Father – why? Why? I look for answers in books. Technicalities. I understand the science. My faith, however, struggles to accept the knowledge. Did you delicately craft him with

Your Creator hands? Then why did the Sovereign's hands take him away? Did You begin a season of new life within me? Then why did You bring about its abrupt end? I rage with questions. Father – why? Silence. That is all I hear now. Are You in the silence? I must trust. Though silent, Your ears are ever hearing.

In my distress I called to the LORD;
I cried to my God for help.
From His temple He heard my voice;
my cry came before Him, into His ears.

(Ps. 18:6)

Father, was it me? Was there something wrong with me? Or was it something I did? They tell me I will be fine. They say that there is nothing medically wrong with me. Perhaps they missed something. Perhaps it is still there. How can I mend it if I don't know where it is? How can I forgive myself, if I don't know for what I'm apologizing? How do I alleviate the guilt, if I am not condemned? I must look beyond my feelings. I must turn to Your truth. You are the creator of life, and You have taken it back in Your wisdom. I need an anchor, or I fear I will simply drift away in my sorrow. Help me, Lord. I want to recuperate. All of me.

The LORD gives strength to His people; the LORD blesses His people with peace.

(Ps. 29:11)

Father, it's church today. Do I have to face the questions? Can I run away from well-meaners? It's too difficult to brave. I want to retreat. Escape. I cannot bear to look at someone else's baby. I dread facing my pregnant friends. Who really understands? Surely I can excuse myself? Save me from fumbling condolences. Save me from having to bridge the awkward silence.

But Jesus often withdrew to lonely places and prayed.

(Luke 5:16)

Lord, I hide in You in this lonely place today, and I pray. Fill me with Your love. With Your love, help me to love Your people as they try to reach out to me. Help me to be loved and cared for. Amen.

Letter One
DEATH

Dear friend,

I suppose I knew in an instant. There was a change in my body, an acute awareness of smells, and a heightened sense of taste. I had a particular dislike for onions. There was a knowing that my body was in preparation, an intimate sixth sense that I was not alone. I was pregnant. It was like that with my first two children as well. All three conceived in passionate abandon, unplanned but wanted. One moment I was going about my daily life, and in the next – a fluttering of consciousness and a flooding of data, and I knew. Instinctively, I put a hand to my tummy and said, 'Hello there, little person. I'm your mummy.'

I suppose you could call that premature. I suppose you could say that I was setting myself up for unnecessary disappointment. In that instant

– it didn't matter. I wholeheartedly entertained both the possibility and the reality that I was a mother again. Charged with a single-minded focus that comes from bearing a new life, I went about the set routine of preparing for another child. Firstly, the pregnancy test kit (although I was convinced I didn't need it). Next, sorting out the matter of which doctor, and which hospital. I needed folic acid, multi-vitamins... and then striking forbidden foods off the shopping list. Calcium – don't forget the calcium! Where were those maternity bras? So glad I kept the awful maternity skirt... I planned my call to my husband, Josh. All systems go. There was no stopping me. I was a mummy again.

I was 'pregnant' for thirteen weeks. In those thirteen weeks, my mind travelled further than the pregnancy ever did. I found out later that the pregnancy didn't make it past the sixth week. There was a pregnancy sac; however, the embryo did not further develop. Whatever the medical details were, I had held a hope of a newborn child for the weeks I believed I was pregnant. I had envisioned the cot, the swaddling, the smell and touch of a newborn. I dreamed about my baby playing with his brother and sister. I felt the swelling of unspeakable joy. We came up with the name 'Sammy' as a sort of unisex name for the baby. And so his presence established itself in our lives and in our hearts. Although I warned myself, like an intermittent alarm, of the possibility of a miscarriage, my love for this child grew.

The day I lost Sammy was like any other pregnant day. It was a Saturday morning, and we had our breakfast as a family. Still feeling quite nauseous, I habitually picked out the nausea-inducing ingredients from my food and semi-consciously processed the 'can eat' and 'should not' eat list. I let out a sigh of relief that the tenuous first trimester was coming to the end.

I walked to the flower market with my two children and passed several white chrysanthemum blooms. A quiet voice within me said, 'You might need these later.' White chrysanthemums are often found in Asian funerals. I semi-brushed the thought off as unnecessary anxiety; however, I grounded myself with the thought, 'You never know what could happen.'

When I arrived home I went to the toilet. In an instant, my pregnancy mode shifted. Spotting. I had read about this; I had imagined what it looked like in my mind. I had prepared myself for the possibility that I could find it in my pregnancy. Here it was, staring me in the face! An unwelcome visitor, its presence was completely beyond my control. Questions raced through my mind: 'Where did it come from? Does the colour matter? Does the volume mean anything? How long should I wait before going to my doctor?' Without telling my husband, I started to forage through my pregnancy books, and swept through the masses of web information. Still my heart could not settle and my mind would not be satisfied. I decided to take the course of action. I told my husband what was happening, and with his encouragement went to our family doctor. The doctor could not decide either way what the spotting meant, without a scan. She advised me to contact my obstetrician. I left without any answers.

I had not yet met my obstetrician. My first appointment with her was the following week. I rang the clinic and spoke with an attending nurse. She asked me a series of questions about the spotting, and fitted me into a cancellation for later that very day. She told me to come down immediately. By now, my adrenaline was surging. I replayed my conversation with the nurse over and over again. What could I pick up from her tone? Was spotting a common query from pregnant mothers? Was it standard protocol to request the mother for an immediate appointment?

We did not raise the alarm to our children, and dropped them off at their grandparents' home. I told them that I needed to see the doctor and check that the baby was well. We said our goodbyes, and Josh and I left. I wasn't sure how my husband was feeling. He seemed calm, yet I wondered if this was to help me feel better. A deadweight, however, had settled in my heart. I was going to find out for sure whether my baby was well or not. I reflected on how this would be our first scan of the baby. We were either going to be elated or devastated.

Before seeing the obstetrician, I went to the toilet again. This time, I prepared myself for the worst. The bleeding was heavier, and fresher blood was seeping out. Just before we went in to see the obstetrician, I placed a hand on Josh's knee and softly said, 'Prepare yourself.' I knew. One look at the scan and the obstetrician knew, too. She started to say, 'It doesn't look good... ' and that was all I needed to hear.

In a short period of time, I had crossed over from jubilation to apprehension, from apprehension to sorrow. The obstetrician's focus shifted to me, counselling me about what to expect as the body aborted the pregnancy sac, telling me not to be afraid at the amount of blood I would witness. She did not offer the procedure Dilation and Curettage (D&C) as an immediate solution, advising me to let my body take its natural course. I wanted to ask, what was natural about losing a baby? I was told that miscarriages were common in early pregnancy, and that it was often the body's way of rejecting a foetus with abnormalities. I wondered what the point was – holding a life within me for a flickering moment, only to have it snuffed out. I wondered if it was my fault. My age, perhaps? Or my health? Screaming inside of me I wanted to know what I could have done to save this child.

I still felt fiercely the instinct to protect my baby. But I sat in silence. I wondered too how my husband felt. And I waited. Waited for the right time to say what I really thought and felt.

I know that there are few known medical facts about miscarriages. I know that it is a common occurrence. I understand that I could not have prevented it. I accept that I may never know why. Though my mind comprehended, my heart did not. All I could do was to cry out to the Lord and lay my heart bare to Him.

My friend, turn to Him. If you are beating yourself up – stop. He would not have you do this. Turn to Him.

Lamenting with you,

Valerie

Letter Two
THE EMPTYING

Dear friend,

I went through a phase which I called 'The Emptying'. My obstetrician advised me that the 'natural' process of miscarriage would look like a heavy period. Although I was hearing her words, I couldn't imagine what was before me. Nothing could have prepared me for the moments I would experience as I watched my body expel the sac within me – an emptying of my womb I could do nothing to stop. I could not even predict when or how. To make matters worse, I didn't know what quantity of blood was considered 'natural' or normal.

I learned later that I haemorrhaged. The blood gushed and poured out of me. Every moment it did, I wondered if this was how I would meet my unborn child. I hated going to the toilet. I dreaded what I would see. I despaired at whether I would be able to face him. Yet I was told to monitor the discharge for tissue material. If the womb did not empty completely I would need a D&C. What a cruel charge. I dreaded going to the toilet and seeing my child for the first time in such gruesome circumstances.

At some point, my husband looked at me and remarked at how pale I had become. We rang our obstetrician, and she told us to go to the Emergency Room at the hospital. I was immediately warded. The nurses spoke ill-tidings to one another with their eyes, although in speech, they tried to console me not to despair until the doctor arrived. I did not know what to expect. The procedure was explained to me in technicalities and I was assured I would not feel pain, nor would I know what was happening to me.

I had to wonder, how would they remove Sammy from me? What would they do to him? Where would he be taken? But I lay there in silence. As they wheeled me into the theatre, I realized I had grown up overnight. I had joined a league of women before me who knew what it was to suffer the loss of an unborn child. My mind wandered to my grandmother who had suffered a miscarriage when young. I wondered why she had never spoken about it. I wondered if there was a realm of unspoken and unheard voices that echoed what I was thinking and feeling. I wished that I could have access to their solace. Again, there was silence.

I was with the medical staff in the theatre. The anaesthetist soothingly whispered, 'It's all right, Valerie, when you wake up it will be all over.' I wanted to believe him. I was about to surrender my body to strangers, and they were about to scrape Sammy out of my womb. Whatever numbness I felt was my way of blocking the overwhelming grief.

Dear friend, I felt so afraid as I was wheeled to the operating theatre. I felt so alone. I did not know what to expect. But I believe our Lord never left my side. I believe He watched with convicted compassion, and unwavering love. The same eyes that watched over me watches over you.

Your friend, *Valerie*

Letter Three
RECUPERATING

Dear friend,

I was sent home to 'recuperate'. The focus was now… me. From the point of the D&C, there was a concerted effort to get me on my feet again. The flowers arrived and the meals and tonics were delivered. There were several helpful offers to mind the children, and to help with the housework. It was as if there was a clanging of gongs, a resounding announcement, 'Don't mention the pregnancy. No mention of the baby. Everybody! Focus on Valerie.' The focus on 'getting well' only served to swell and suffocate me. I wanted so badly to push back the closing walls of this new focus. I was not done grieving. I was not done letting go of my baby. I was not ready to recuperate.

Closer to the truth, I was not yet relieved of my torment – was it my fault? I felt like a broken machine that had not yet proved that it was worth fixing. Nevertheless, I went along with everybody else. I played the dutiful 'patient'. Convalescing left me to my own private thoughts, and it seemed silly to voice them to the world that was desperate to move on. And so the chapter seemed to end, and I prepared myself to return to normal life.

But normality did not return. The doctor told me to expect a 'heavier than usual' period after the D&C, as the uterus shed its lining. What I didn't expect was the physical after-effects of my loss. I continued to be reminded that I had lost my child as my body expelled whatever was left in my womb. My body, though recuperating from the haemorrhage, was not done with the miscarriage. I continued to experience painful abdominal cramps while nursing a lingering morning sickness. Strangely, I didn't want to let go of the morning sickness. Although a nuisance prior to the miscarriage, it was now the only presence (and perhaps evidence) of my pregnancy.

I found it difficult to sit through the cramps. I was told to expect this as the uterus contracted to its normal size. The cramps were an agonizing, uncontrollable sensation. They were the same sort of cramps I experienced after delivering my other two babies. When I had my two living children, I welcomed the sensation. I marvelled at my machine-body contracting the womb after finishing its work. With a newborn baby in your arms, you are pleasantly distracted by the finished 'product'. Nuzzling your newborn, locked in the raptures of new love, the sensations fade into the background. What's more, I could congratulate myself on a job well done. The forty-week baby factory was closing for business after successful production!

This time, I felt defective somehow. I felt like some authority greater than me had decided to shut down my factory without explaining it to me, without forewarning. I was not given the chance to defend myself. I was in my thirties; I was not past my expiry date yet! From the moment I recognized I was pregnant, I reduced my caffeine, avoided risky foods, took my vitamins... But, the linings of my womb continued to be stripped away. The remnants of evidence that a life was within me was being emptied. I could not control this. It was beyond me. The only form of control I felt I could exercise was to try to find an explanation of what had happened to my pregnancy.

Thanks to the information age, you can search on the Internet for the term 'miscarriage' and get hundreds of results. Some of the websites were medical and some were personal stories. I was ushered into the technicalities of what I had experienced – definitions, symptoms, causes and statistics. I foraged the lists for what I could have done that caused it, and found no answers. The next best explanation was that there was something 'defective' (as put by the medical sites) with the baby. I found it hard to accept this. Why would God plant a defective seed in me?

Dear friend, this was the point I had to trust *Abba* Father. I had to cling on to Scripture and will myself to find assurance in His wisdom and sovereignty. He is in control. He who spun the stars into being, who weaves life and death into His plan – *He knew*. He hears your questions.

He has the answers, although He may be silent. We can know that silence is for our good, and in line with His purpose. Rest in this knowledge, my friend.

In the darkness with you,

Valerie

Letter Four
TRUTH TELLING

Dear friend,

I have almost always told my two children the truth. I may have slipped up when asked if there was any more ice cream in the freezer, but for the most part, I tell the truth. It's something I believe in, strongly. I confess, I am one of those mothers who told her children that Santa was a man in a red suit who worked for the shopping centre. However, I also proceeded to tell them the story of St Nicholas, the man, and the message of love he represented. I try to avoid empty promises, making sure my words bear the gravity of truth. To me, my words need to represent an uncompromising front. A certainty, a reliability.

Yet I wavered with the miscarriage. When we found out I was pregnant, Josh and I talked about whether we would wait until the second trimester to tell the children. We acknowledged that a miscarriage was possible, and saving the news for more certain times would be prudent. However, I felt rather sick from the pregnancy, and we thought the children would wonder at why I wasn't playing with them, or showing enthusiasm for their morning antics. I thought they might worry about me ducking in and out of the bathroom to throw up. We convinced ourselves that we would be able weather the storm should a miscarriage happen, and joyfully announced to our children that they were going to have a new baby brother or sister.

Once we had decided to tell them, we didn't wait too long. That day, at the dinner table, my husband began with, 'Children, we have some good news!' He paused only to beam at me, and then told them. The children were thrilled – ecstatically so! They didn't stop to ask how it had happened; instead, they demanded to know whether it was a boy or a girl. It wasn't fair you see, because it meant that one of them would have the same-sex playmate, and the other would be left out. They merrily chatted about how they would feed and bathe the baby, and where the new addition would sleep.

I thoroughly enjoyed watching my children's excitement. As a mother, a new child in your womb brings about a tender anticipation for the fledgling you will nurse and grow at your bosom. For my children, they were simply filled with the joy of one more to add to their bedroom, someone smaller to fuss over, and an expectant change of their status to 'older' brother or sister. I was happy for them. I thought a great deal about what it meant for them to have a sibling. I hoped that whether or not they married, they would have each other to witness their life unfold. I hoped that they would have a constant companion, supporter, documenter, and advisor. They would not be alone; they would have each other.

So when we learned that the baby had not developed in my womb, I wanted to hide the truth from them. I was just coming to terms with it myself; I didn't know how they would. They had not experienced death before. Josh and I briefly discussed what we would do. There was little to discuss, really. We knew we would have to tell them.

When we returned from the hospital, we picked them up from their grandparents' house. They knew we had been to the 'baby doctor', but they didn't know the reason why. They were full of questions about whether we had seen the baby on the ultrasound, and what the doctor said. They were still so joyful. This was probably the first time I felt disconnected from their world. I had just crossed the chasm to sorrow, and they were still on the other side.

We arrived home and gathered once more at the dining table. Again, it was my husband who announced the news. I can't remember exactly what he said. I do remember having a running commentary in my head: 'Is this the right thing to do? Should we tell them? What terms would we use? How would we tell them, so that they could understand the complete end of the pregnancy?' In the end I decided to use 'death' as an explanation. I don't know if it was the best way to convey 'miscarriage' to them. I did think it would reflect the loss we as a family would feel. When it was my turn to speak, I told the children that the baby was sick, and he died. My son's instant reaction was of anger. He said, 'I told you not to jiggle about so much. You should have eaten healthy food.' My daughter responded with a question, 'Can we buy another baby?' In steadier times, I would have taken in their complete innocence with awe and delight. That day, however, it rattled me. I didn't know how to respond to my son's anger. Rationally I knew he was coming to terms with the emotions he felt, and in an attempt to gain control, he chastised me. Perhaps his words reflected the ambiguity I felt. I was not yet sure it wasn't my fault, somehow. My daughter's response brought about a sense of guilt. I felt I had led her down a path only to blockade it, and I could not help her.

It didn't stop there. More questions. Where did the baby go? How did the doctor take it out? Did you see the baby? Why didn't you see the baby? It was too much for me. I knew they were hurting in their childlike way. But I needed to retreat, emotionally and physically. And so I did. The days that passed were slow. The children would ask, and I would garner whatever strength I had to process their feelings and confusion with them, trying not to lose my composure as I did – not to break down myself. And then I would retreat into my personal grief. Finally, when their minds were satisfied, the questions subsided. A solemnity pervaded the home. We grieved together. As a family, we crossed over from jubilation to mourning.

My friend, you may not have these exact circumstances yourself. Perhaps you might think that I ought to be consoled that I do at least have living children. You are probably right. Somehow, though, there was a disconnection for me between my living and my dead. Sammy was a deeper loss for me because I never held him. I was struggling to let him go when I didn't have anything to cling on to. The presence of my children, although it brought gratitude that they were alive, also brought sadness to know they had lost someone too.

In honesty,

Valerie

Letter Five
HERE COMES THE RAIN

Dear friend,

There was a night I could not sleep. Josh was soundly resting. I checked in on the children; they were resting too. There were no more emails or text messages of condolences. I had two very close friends, Kath and Amelie, whom I had not informed about the miscarriage. Amelie had miscarried several years back, and I remembered her anger, confusion and hurt at the time. As I thought of my friends, and as I felt the cramps in my stomach, for the first time, I cried a torrent of tears. Here is an extract of what I wrote to them:

Firstly, Kath, I think you are away, so don't feel bad when you read this, I can already picture you by the computer with cyber hugs :)

Secondly, Amelie, you were the first person

I thought of when I knew for sure about the miscarriage... strange that everything you said back then and everything I said to you came back in a rush. It's almost as if you were there to tell me what to think and how to feel.

It's midnight, the kids are in bed, I don't have to be a mum. Josh is in bed, and the one visitor has gone home. I can put away all those roles and just be sad for me.

Not really sure why I am sad. Medically I did not develop past the 5th week, so technically there wasn't a 'baby' per se. I suppose I grieve for the life that was, and the possibility. For most of the day I was sad for Josh and the kids. Then I was sad for our friends as they tried to respond. Remember, Amelie, when you talked about the ways people had to deal with their own issues when they tried to comfort you?

Me. Well, I get to have the visuals of a miscarriage as it discharges itself and all the bodily sensations of being emptied. I can't exactly switch it off and distract myself.

As for God, not angry with Him, only wonder

why He waited 13 weeks? Or, if it was just a living shell for 13 weeks? Still, I know Him well enough to know that the outcome will be better than what I can anticipate.

Don't think I will go to church tomorrow.

Since writing, the tears have stopped! It was good to say what really was going through my mind. Thank you ladies...

Love, Val

What follows are some excerpts from their immediate replies, which ministered to and touched me profoundly:

From Amelie:

Oh Val! I'm so sorry. I am sitting here crying too.

I wish I could be there to hug you right now.

I will be praying for you and Josh.

For me, the grief has eased with time, but is still there I guess. It really helped us, after time had passed, to have a kind of funeral service. But, as we know, everyone has a different way of grieving. I know that the 'baby' hadn't developed, but I had loved it for 20 weeks like a potential person. I think I may have written our baby a letter too – it made me cry, but the tears were good.

From Kath:

Val... don't know what to say. All I really want to do is be there with you and sit silently, allowing you to say or do what you need to.

The tears are good, they need to come, but you know that already. The talking is necessary too, that I can vouch for from experience. If you need physical comfort from Josh just tell him. I get the feeling that you just want to sit, hug and cry for a bit. It's hard keeping it all together for everyone else when all you really want to do is break down and let someone else pick up the pieces and tell you it's OK. I'd love to talk to you, or rather let you talk to me. So please let us know when [it's] a good time... to call. If you'd rather not talk though, that's OK too. All in good time. My prayers are with you, Josh and the kids – all three of them.

These ladies knew me, and their concern was for my world that was crashing in on me. They were giving me permission to grieve. To cry. To say that I wasn't OK, and to ask for comfort. Nobody else had said this. Kath even affirmed my pregnancy as one of three; she named him – a child of mine. I wept as I read their replies. I had permission to grieve.

The truth is, I felt embarrassed for the fool I had been. For entertaining the image of my third child. For even calling 'it' a 'child'. Secretly I had planned the nursery. The details flooded my mind each day. Where to put the crib? How would I hear the cry? Where would I sit to nurse? As the details filled my mind, my heart was bursting with anticipation. Even if I played the game of silence for the first trimester, who could have stopped my heart from loving? Who could have prevented me from hoping? Who could have curbed my longing? How could I have stifled my rejoicing? A gift! A child is a gift from God Himself, straight from heaven into your arms. A conjoining with the Creator Himself.

Dear friend, do you have someone you can speak to? Don't feel foolish to voice your thoughts and feelings. There is no shame in grieving your loss. There is no shame in having loved your child. I pray your tears find their way. I pray you have an empathic ear from those you decide to share with.

In the rain, with you,

Valerie

Letter Six
HIDING

Dear friend,

I sat on my bed, unwilling to face the day before me. I felt such dread in my heart, it held me paralyzed. It was Sunday. On any other Sunday I wore with eagerness my triple hat of pastor's wife, mother, and fellow worshipper in Christ. At other stormy periods in life, like a homing pigeon, I ran to my heavenly Father's house. However, on this particular Sunday, I was torn... I wanted to be embraced by His Word and His people, but it would be the first time since the miscarriage that I would have to face the church.

As I imagined what lay before me, it was as if I was entering a minefield. I could not control who would greet me, avoid me, or tiptoe around me. Worst still, I could not predict what would be said to me. I was not even sure if I knew what

I needed to hear from the people around me. Mixed in with the dread were feelings of shame. After all, despite what the medical books said, I still felt as if I had not been able to carry my baby to term. I was also embarrassed, as so many knew about my pregnancy. Mostly I felt anguished and terribly vulnerable. I found it difficult to trust my pain to others. I did not want to rub shoulders with anyone, for I knew my bleeding heart was intricately woven on my sleeve that day. I would not be able to shield it, hide it, or protect it.

In my fog, I rang a friend and explained my predicament over whether or not to go to church. She said, 'I have been thinking about you all morning. I knew you would be turning the question over in your head.' Instantly I was brought into the warm embrace of timely empathy. How did she know what I was thinking? Where did she find the ability to reach deep into her heart to connect with my pain? As I spoke with her, she turned and tossed the worries and the uncertainties with me. She had no answer for me, but she understood, and she shared my turmoil.

Her empathic response gave me a hope.

Perhaps God had prepared her for my phone call. Perhaps He could do the same with others. I prayed to the Lord and poured out my conflicted feelings. On the one hand a desire to be enveloped by love from my heavenly family. On the other hand a deep fear that they would disappoint me. I searched in my heart for all the scripture I could remember, and for all the Christian values I could muster. Then came His Spirit to galvanize my soul. His body was given for me for the forgiveness of sin, and His church given to me for fellowship until He comes again. I decided that the body of Christ was there for mutual encouragement and growth, in good times and in bad. I needed to be loved and prayed for. They needed to care and express their faith in love.

I resolved that I would take the step. Whether I would find comfort or pain, I believed Jesus would be there with me. I prayed for courage, and I prayed most of all for love. I prayed that I would be able to love, even in my sorrow. I was going to church.

Little did I know that the next decision would be as crippling as the first. What was I going to wear? Would it be offensive to put on something fitting, to show an empty cocoon? Would it be misleading to wear something loose? Should I wear black as a sign of mourning, or would that seem ridiculous? I almost gave up. Too hard! Yet, resolving to follow through on my decision, I put on an outfit that was loose-fitting but held in with a belt. A good enough compromise. I put on my make-up (so my children wouldn't think it was different from any other Sunday) and went to church.

I wish I could tell you it was smooth sailing. The Lord did not silence the inappropriate comments, nor did He stave off the awkward floundering. He did, however, fortify the loving touches and the respectful silences into a wall of comfort and companionship around me. I felt as if I was walking through the crowds in His sandals. I arrived at a profound understanding of how our Lord might have felt as He rode the roller-coaster of adulation and disdain from the very people He had come to save and love. I had a brief flicker of insight into the suffering servant who took Himself away from the crowds to pray as His imminent sorrow approached. Yet He continued to walk, to teach, to serve and to love. This was His hand holding me steady in the boat while the waves rocked about. And it was His hand that steadied my heart to go through whatever hurt or confusion I might have felt. I looked up to Him in that mixed time of grief and joy, and I silently thanked Him.

My friend, I do not know if you will have the same fears when it is your turn to face the crowds. How I wish I could be with you as you take in that first sharp breath and walk into the limelight of well-meaning concern. Yet I know that there is One who understands the loneliness of grief and sorrow and being pressed by the multitude far better than I do. I must leave you with Him, because He will know what you need, and in what way your courage will come. Take the time you need to have your solace, and when it comes to facing the crowds, I pray you plunge with the daring abandon of one who knows He will be there to catch you – at just the right moment.

Below is a personal glossary I have written for you of things that were said to me, both helpful and unhelpful. I hope it takes the edge off that first step.

HELPFUL

Silence and big hugs

Silence and tears

People letting me know they had prayed for me that day

Friends who rang my husband to pray with him

UNHELPFUL

Friends who never acknowledged the miscarriage (but knew about it) by avoiding the topic

Survivor stories implying that I would be fine too

Comments such as: 'Perhaps that was a practise run; you can always try again', 'There must have been something wrong with the baby', 'Never mind this loss, now you can have fun trying again', 'Maybe God knew two children would be enough for you.'

If I am honest, I have not forgotten the comments, and can vividly recall the messengers, although I have forgiven the well-meaning folk who delivered the remarks. I do believe they were meant in love and backed up with prayer, which our Father understood.

Take courage my friend, Valerie

Letter Seven
TAKING CONTROL

Dear friend,

In April, three months after I lost Sammy, I made a hasty decision. I signed up for two years of gym membership, complete with a personal trainer. All my life I have loathed exercise. I was not much of a sportswoman in school. I entertained the occasional leisurely walk, but would not aspire to perspiration. Although I had miscarried some months ago, and although I was told by my doctor that I could resume my daily activities after two weeks without consequence, I was still feeling physically weak. I did not feel I had regained my strength or vigour. I was tired of feeling impotent. I wanted to regain my health. I wanted some semblance of control over my body. I couldn't will it into shape, so I decided to enlist help.

The shopping centre where I bought my groceries had on its seventh floor a modern, fully equipped gym. I took the plunge, went up the escalator, and was immediately ushered into a cold and intimidating environment. There were sculpted bodies everywhere. I felt completely and utterly out of place. I was assigned my personal trainer soon after signing up as a member. The young man was built like a tank. He smiled cordially, and began asking me a series of health-related questions. I wasn't sure what I needed to divulge, and casually mentioned that I had recently recovered from a miscarriage. He was visibly affected by this. He shuffled his papers uncomfortably, and stuttered out the next question.

As a therapist, I have a bad habit of switching into therapy mode at the drop of a hat. I can't bear to see someone else feel uncomfortable because of something I have said. I was acutely aware of his discomfort, and tried to minimize whatever pain I might have been feeling at the time. I continued to explain my health circumstances, and concentrated on telling him how the miscarriage had left me feeling in physical limbo. I was still wearing the pregnancy weight, and I felt weaker than I was accustomed to. I told him that my goal was not to look like the next super-model, but to feel in control of my health.

My personal trainer turned out to be a wonderful support to me. Although we did not talk about the miscarriage again, he had a gentle and respectful approach to our sessions. He was reassuring and kind in his manner, and firmly but gently helped me grow in confidence in regaining strength. He did not talk to me about losing weight. He spoke determinedly about building my strength, sleeping well again, and feeling vital. The wonderful thing was, he was a Christian. We spoke about the Lord, church, family, as if we were old friends. Unbeknown to him, he ministered to me in my hour of need.

Every time I got on the treadmill, I uttered in my mind, 'Never again! I will never again feel out of control of my body.' When I felt like stopping out of exhaustion, I would say, 'For Sammy. I need to do this for Sammy.' I was trying to ascertain if it was my health that had caused his death. Not only was I at the gym twice a week,

I sent myself for a full medical check-up. I was looking for an answer. More to the point, I was looking for some control; some rational way to make sense of my loss and to make sure it never happened again.

I started to lose weight, and my personal trainer was ecstatic. He had not seen such quick results before. It was probably due to the fact that I pushed myself to my physical limit. After our sessions, I stayed back for an additional half hour on my own to do more. However, this ushered in a fresh wounding. I was losing my pregnant shape. My last tangible reminder, proof even, that Sammy existed. I felt torn. I wasn't sure if I was ready to let go. I silently nursed my grief, and obediently pushed through with my training.

My friend, I think my attempts at gaining control were a way of punishing myself. If the Father remained silent, if I couldn't appease myself with medical facts that it wasn't my fault, I thought I deserved misery. Yet I also wanted to be healed, and move on. It would be a very long time before I stopped looking for answers.

After several checks, I was assured that I was in good health. Perhaps you are not yet there; be kind to yourself. You are not to blame.

Hoping for you,

Valerie

Letter Eight
SHARING AN UMBRELLA

Dear friend,

You may have noticed how solitary my grief has been up to this point. Though I have mentioned my husband, I have not mentioned how he felt through this ordeal. That is because I did not ask him at first. For a long time I felt that the sorrow belonged to my body. Although both my husband and I were involved in conceiving our child, I felt that I alone had lost him. It was my body that had expelled our child. I thought that while our joy was shared, and augmented by our individual hopes and dreams, the anguish of letting go was wholly mine to bear.

Many times I tried to talk to him. Somehow, I couldn't get the words out. I didn't know how to begin. As the months rolled on, I thought it would be a burden on his part to reopen old wounds. He seemed to have moved on. Life resumed, we went about our daily routines as we did before. We did not utter a word about trying for another child; I suppose Josh knew I would broach the subject when I was ready. He remained attentive. He didn't turn away from me. He didn't close his heart to me – but I closed my heart to him. I sealed off that part of me which was still hurting and vulnerable. Perhaps I hoped that the sadness would somehow dissolve on its own, thus absolving me from whatever lingering guilt or reprehension I felt.

The truth is, the guilt, the grief, the anguish, seeped into my everyday life. I reached a point of exhaustion from denying expression to my true feelings. It ate into my relationship with my husband. I expressed my secondary grievances, only to be frustrated with the outcomes. I thought I was burnt-out from the housework, juggling jobs, ministry roles and children. In actuality, I was probably shattered from carrying the burden of our loss myself.

I think my heavenly Father knew this and one day, by divine arrangement, sent a counsellor our way. He suggested that my husband and I meet him for a private chat. I had expected to talk about our domestic issues, and to iron out some of our communication challenges. However, this dear gentleman looked gravely at me and enquired about the miscarriage. He wanted to know how I felt. He wanted to know how I had endured the loss. Most strikingly, he asked both of us how we had grieved together. His point was that if it took both of us to make a baby, it would take both of us to grieve and complete the healing process. I was stunned. As I spoke to him, and as I expressed to my husband my deepest feelings that day, I wept afresh, as if I had only just miscarried.

It didn't stop there. When we returned home, Josh looked me fully in the eyes and told me he hadn't realized what I had been feeling. He urged me to tell him everything. He wanted to know; he didn't want me to censor anything. I poured out my heart that night. I wept and wept, and probably for the first time, expressed myself in totality. He shared with me how he had felt. He told me his hopes for the baby, and how they had turned to sorrow after the loss. He expressed his deepest desires for his unborn child. I felt that although it had been raining in my heart for a long time, sharing my grief with him was akin to standing under an umbrella and taking shelter for awhile.

My friend, have you taken shelter with someone yet? Our faithful Father hears our cries. He has also given us the fellowship of family and believers that we can turn to in times of difficulty. It might not stop the rain completely, or prevent the tears from falling again. It may, however, ease the pain for a moment. Just enough for you to breathe in and exhale, and feel the warmth of companionship. I pray for you today, that you will find the warmth of an inviting umbrella to stand under.

Waiting in the shelter for you,

Valerie

LOOKING BACK ON *Letter Nine*

I have tried as best as possible not to interfere with the writing of the letters as they were written. They are an intact representation of what I was thinking and feeling while veiled in grief. However, reading Letter Nine again, it struck me that there is a sudden shift in my writing which makes it sound like I woke up one day and the grief left me. I am not sure if this was the case, although I do remember writing the letter waiting for the tears to well up, for the sadness to descend upon me, and then realizing that I was feeling peace instead. I do think there was a gradual healing that started to take place after I spoke my true feelings to my husband, Josh. I confronted other emotions, not just grief. I was angry with him. I was angry that he had seemingly moved on and left me behind. It wasn't so much that I believed he side-stepped Sammy. It was more that he seemed to have return to 'normal', and I had lost his companionship in my sorrow. I arrived at this conclusion because I watched Josh throw himself into his work. Being a pastor, I thought he was out the door to help everyone else, and he seemed back on track. I was hurt, I was angry, I was resentful. I had not articulated this to him. As a result, without realizing it, I shut off a part of my heart from him. I was also scared. I was afraid that the miscarriage had therefore fundamentally shifted our relationship, and we were living in some sort of warped parallel universe. That is, we were living together, participating in the same events, and yet experiencing two separate emotional realities.

The counsellor I mentioned in the previous letter would not let me push these emotions aside. Each time I tried to move on to focus on our domestic issues (we were facing quite a bit of conflict at the time), this lovely gentleman would steer the conversation back to the miscarriage. He explained that we had to grieve together. Somehow we had to turn to face one another and, as he put it, in stormy times, we needed to find shelter and safety in one another.

Josh explained to me that he was coping with his grief too. Losing Sammy was something he could not fix. He expressed his anguish at watching me lose a baby. He shared that he was nursing a lost dream, too. So he did the next best thing to help him gain control – he worked. In his own way, it helped him feel like he was doing something for me, for our kids, for our family. I accessed Joshua's sorrow that night and our honesty brought about a unity. Then I began to heal.

I would also like to add that the month Sammy was due was a very hard month for me. I did not write about it because it brought much pain. I threw myself into other writing projects and took a break from this collection. I cried a lot that month. I cannot remember the due date now, but I can tell you that the due date, at the time, was indelibly engraved in my mind and heart. It was made all the more difficult because a friend of mine who fell pregnant the same time as I did had her beautiful little girl. I kept thinking about how it would have been me, too.

How much I wanted to have a baby to hold, to nurse, to love. I think for me, acknowledging this ache and longing helped me to heal as well. I started to think about having another baby, and I started to look forward, rather than look back.

Letter Nine
OVER THE RAINBOW

Dear friend,

I received news about seedling babies growing in mothers' wombs today. I inhaled the perfume of their mothers' joy and anticipation, and my heart glowed for them. My heart did not ache today. I had dreaded seeing pictures of the newborns born in Sammy's month. I held back secret tears as I congratulated my friends who had given birth in that same period. The thing about this high technology world is that there isn't an envelope to hide the images so you can tuck them away for another season. They simply appear at the most unexpected moments.

Today, however, I warmed to the dimpled faces and duckling hair of other people's babies. There was no sting in my heart. This was another instance of change. One day seems like such a small shift in time, but a monumental shift in my heart had occurred. The day I lost Sammy, I breathed in sorrow. But I exhaled today.

I tried to pinpoint what exactly had changed. Where did the aching go? How did it disappear? Was it because the busyness of life took over? Did I simply forget? Then came the prick of a doubting conscience. Was I minimizing the last months of grief? Maybe it was silly of me to have wallowed in it. Then came the rational side. Perhaps there was some kind of gestational countdown that lingered after the miscarriage. Some kind of tick-tocking until the fortieth week. This did not satisfy me. I reminded myself that this was my personal grief. A path carved by my heavenly Father, no doubt to shape me and mould me. With that I exhaled again. Perhaps it was just time, the right time.

My dear friend, I do not know when this time will come for you. I cannot say if it will dawn on you in the same way it did for me. This I know. Our God holds and understands the seasons of our hearts, and knows the exact moment to soothe that sting. Swiftly, I hope, for you.

Waiting to exhale with you, *Valerie*

Letter Ten
ONE YEAR ON

Dear friend,

We have just passed our one year mark since we lost Sammy. I now speak of it as 'the pregnancy' or 'the miscarriage', like an event that occurred and passed in the normal track of time. Nothing unusual, nothing tragic. Just an event. I think this means the grief is passing, or has passed. It is hard for me to say for sure. I no longer feel the shroud of sorrow engulfing me. Nor do I have the lingering desire to hold on to a memory quickly fading.

When did I start to heal? As I read my letters to you, I am struck by how many of the details I have now forgotten. I do not feel the grief in my body. The memory of Sammy lives in my heart, but I do not ache at the thought of him. In fact, there is a longing now. A renewed hope that I might conceive again. I am not afraid of this thought. I was, for a long time. Now, the thought of being pregnant again grips me with excitement. I peer into prams for a glimpse of a bundled baby. I turn in the direction of a newborn's cry, and linger to hear its unique melody. The nursery of my mind is open again. In it I see the crib with white lace, the nursing chair with the crocheted afghan and neatly folded white napkins ready for use. It is a bright room, filled with hope.

I wanted to share a moment with you. A good moment. I was talking to a friend the other day, catching up on the various events that took place in the last year. The miscarriage was shared as one of the events that had occurred. I reported it as part of a string of happenings over the year. Although I paused in my mind to give a moment of respect for my loss, I did not think much about the reaction I would get; I did not expect to be understood or consoled. Yet this dear friend, half an hour later, quietly said to me, 'I am really very sorry about the miscarriage' and gave me a gentle touch on my arm. I thanked her, and we moved on to other topics. This was a good moment for me, for several reasons.

First, I realized that I had integrated my loss as one part of the many things that had happened to me in the year. It did not stand out on its own any more. Secondly, I was not dependent on the reaction of another person to validate the event as justified grief. Thirdly, I was given a moment of grace – there were other women who reacted with a measure of feeling that was not different from my own. This lady shared my grief, even if it had passed; she responded from her heart, how she would have felt if it happened to her. Lastly, I felt soothed and cared for by her empathy. I was able to receive her care. This last reason was especially important to me. If my wound was not healing, or even healed, I would have cringed at anybody's attempt to reach out and soothe it, for fear that it would sting all the more.

I suppose this is the point where our journeys might have taken a different course. I do not know what your life has become since you lost your baby. I do not know if you returned to the same life, or if you took another path; or if you have had a 'good moment' that has helped you move on. I do know that the constancy of our Father in heaven is a certainty. He will not leave you groping in the dark. I hope you are in a space where your mind and heart find some light; if not a lot, then enough for a glimpse of a hopeful tomorrow.

Finally, my friend, I can tell you that as I write this letter, I no longer blame myself. I have accepted my miscarriage as it was, an unfortunate loss. I have lived through the grief; the rain in my heart has stopped, and I can finally see the rainbow. The rainbow of hope. Of a promise that He is indeed faithful. He never left.

May you know that He is near to you,

Valerie

Letter Eleven
DREAMING

Dear friend,

Do you have several photograph albums at home? Do you recall with exact detail each and every picture? Or do you have a few favourites that your mind's eye recalls with ease, and with pleasure? The photos you took last week are probably still vivid in your mind. You will know at what time you took them, the circumstances surrounding each one, and the exact location of all the other people who were not in the photographs. However, if I were to ask you about these details a year later, you would not be able to recall them. You probably would not remember the picture, unless it was of particular sentimental value.

I feel the same way today about the miscarriage. This is my last letter to you, simply because for me, the memory of it has faded. I believe I have passed through the grief. Although Sammy holds a precious place in my heart, it is a quiet place. My heart is silent with respect for his existence. It simply holds him there with little consequence to how I feel.

I have changed, though. In my person. Because I encountered death, I was awoken to life. I became grateful that I was alive, that the people I loved were alive. I began to cherish the moments I had with them. I want to say the things I have held back, to speak what I feel, and to dream with driven passion.

This is what I have written recently to friends, on reflection, seventeen months after the miscarriage:

I can't remember a time when I haven't nursed a secret dream. When I was five, I imagined I was the princess of my nursery school. At seven, I wanted to be a singer. By age ten, I got more status conscious, and it was a doctor that I would become. Puberty struck, and I found altruism, I wanted to be a music teacher. In my late teens, I read

Ecclesiastes, and I was passionate about becoming a missionary. When I graduated, I was reading Elisabeth Elliot and the story of her martyred missionary husband, and I thought I would change the world with some super combination of psychology and theology. I can't remember a time I haven't dreamed.

Over time, my dreaming became more 'out there', but my tolerance of risk remained low. Daughter of a banker, you see, I tended to see the security of a vault and the solidarity of a balanced sheet. But a pair of Crocs, and a tragic loss, changed all of this. One day, I was dreaming. It was the time when Crocs first came out, with the basic look and shape. They looked ugly to me, but the concept intrigued me. I said to someone, 'Wouldn't it be great if someone invented Glamour Crocs?' (By this I meant work shoes, or evening shoes made out of the same material). The person turned to me, screwed their face and said, 'Who would buy Glamour Crocs?' Now, by this time, I had already looked up the Crocs website, and investigated patents, and looked up production in China. After that one comment, I turned back to my reality, and put that baby to sleep.

Then, there WAS a baby. A pregnancy. I was pregnant for a very brief period, and I had a dream. This time, a dream of a baby. He was curly-haired, and followed me everywhere in this dream. He wore a blue jump-suit and had a turned-up button nose. I asked the baby, 'Why are you following me everywhere?' A voice answered the question, but it was not the voice of the baby. The voice said, 'He follows you wherever you go... he will bring you great joy.' I lost that pregnancy not long after. The dream seemed like a cruel joke, and the voice seemed to have mocked me.

However, that pain stirred up a passion. Bringing together all of my convictions as a Christian, a wife, and a mother to a blistering, bubbling, boil. I began to write a book about my miscarriage, in the form of letters to an unnamed mother. But my grief had not finished, and so the book could not move very far. For a while I stopped writing these letters. It was too hard. My radar for life, though, was very much active, having just tasted loss. And I delved into the inner world of children with greater sensitivity and curiosity. I saw them as a miraculous gift of life. I wondered how our heavenly Father could give such precious gifts to us. I knew all too well that these lives did not come with certainty. After all, not every pregnancy results in a child born! What remarkable responsibility we had as stewards of these lives! Not just as [mothers] but as individuals in society. So, I took leave from my book documenting my grief in the miscarriage, and I began to write for life! I wrote for little lives, and little souls. My first children's book was completed and published, and when I held the printed copy for the first time, my husband congratulated me on the birth of our third child! I cried when he said this. Because to me, that was the most wonderful thing anybody could have said to me. I did have a baby in blue! He does follow me around! He does bring me exceedingly great joy. It was the birthing of a book, and a realization of a dream.

With all my affection,

Valerie

Letter Twelve
TO MY BELOVED SAMMY

Dear Sammy,

I dreamt about you once. The only pregnant dream I had of you. You had the curliest hair, a cute button nose and a sweet disposition. Yet, somehow, you seemed to be able to look straight at me and fuse with my thoughts. In my dream you followed me wherever I went. Up and down the stairs, into the laundry, then to the kitchen, through the hurricane mess of crayons, toys and books. You seemed to be right with me, around every mundane corner of my everyday life. I asked you why you were following me. I don't think you answered me in my dream. But I heard His voice. There is clarity to the familiarity of the shepherd's voice. Still, quiet, and yet resounding through my consciousness: 'This child follows you wherever you go. He will bring you great joy.' Then, just like that you disappeared from my mind. I woke up in the morning turning the dream over in my head. I wondered at what it meant. I accepted that you were a precious gift who would bring great joy not only to me, but to our whole family.

After you left, that dream seemed like a cruel joke. There was very little joy when I thought of you, Sammy. I tried my best to forget you. I do not know your scent, I cannot picture your form, nor can I trace your voice in my memories. Yet, I cannot seem to forget you. You are fused with me. I just know – you. In that way, you follow me wherever I go.

This last year I have sought so far, so deep and so wide in Jesus. I have asked so many questions of Him. Some answered, some not. All that I have endeavoured to do has meant so much more. I have treasured life this year; mine, your father's, and your siblings'. I have become all the more dependent on His mercies for the little and the big. Each time I think of you, it gives me the courage to jump higher, run faster, dive deeper and soar further. You gave me a renewed sense of life, because I was confronted with your death and my loss.

A friend of mine said that when she lost her baby, she mused whether or not she would see him in heaven. A kindly minister did not have a sure answer for her, but he surmised that if life existed in the womb, then her child could be with our Father. Though I am not sure about this as fact, I am comforted by the thought. I might see you and get an eternal opportunity to love you. When I'm in heaven, I reckon I will be looking out for you, Sammy. You may have missed out on knowing your family in the physical realm, but perhaps you will know us in the spiritual.

In many ways, you are the blessed one, Sammy. You do not need to know suffering; you do not need to feel pain. You will not have to shed a tear or live with unanswered questions. Your reality is the one we long for. One where you are able to be next to the Father, and know only perfection, beauty and love. I am again comforted by this. I have great joy thinking on it. I have not given you sagely words in this life, but allow me to say this: Worship Him, Sammy, and save a place for me, next to you.

With all my love.

LOSING
SAMMY
Valerie Theng